Lemon and Tortilla Soup

Vegetable Manchow Soup

SANJEEV KAPOOR'S
SIMPLY VEGETARIAN
Recipes for the Indian Kitchen

Soups & Salads

SANJEEV KAPOOR'S
SIMPLY VEGETARIAN
Recipes for the Indian Kitchen

Soups & Salads

In association with Alyona Kapoor

Popular
Prakashan

POPULAR PRAKASHAN PVT. LTD.

© 2004 by Sanjeev Kapoor

First Published 2004

(3882)

ISBN - 81-7991-134-9

PRINTED IN INDIA
By Thomson Press (I) Ltd.
18/35 Milestone, Delhi Mathura Road, Faridabad (Haryana)
and Published by Ramdas Bhatkal
for Popular Prakashan Pvt. Ltd.

Exclusively Distributed by : Impulse Marketing

Dedication

To all the lovers of authentic
food whose enthusiasm makes us
dig deeper into the
Khazana of Khana, and come up
with what is best
and most precious in cuisine.

Acknowledgements

A.I. Kazi

Afsheen Panjwani

Anand Bhandiwad

Mrs. Lata Lohana & Capt. K. K. Lohana

Debashish Mukherjee

Dhiraj Bolur

Drs. Meena & Ram Prabhoo

Ganesh Pednekar

Harpal Singh Sokhi

Jijesh Gangadharan

Jyotsna & Mayur Dvivedi

Kishore Roy

Mallika Shetty

Manish Anand

Namita Pusalkar

Namrata & Sanjiv Bahl

Neelima Acharya
Neena Murdeshwar
Pallavi Sharma
Pooja & Rajeev Kapoor
Priti Surve
Rajeev Matta
Rutika Samtani
Sanjay Bakshi
Satish Parab
Shivani Ganesh
Smeeta Bhatkal
Swapna Shinde
Tripta Bhagattjee
Vinayak Gawande

Note to the Readers

There exists a food that binds the universe! It is soup. You may be in any part of the world and be sure to find out about the local soup, broth, gruel, consommé or *shorba*! A soup is a soup and is just as nourishing called by any other name.

In fact, soup is as old as cooking itself. Adapted and reinvented through the centuries it is the ultimate in creativity encompassing an astounding range of textures, flavours, ingredients and character. It can be served as an appetizer, or as a one-course meal or as a snack, it is stylish whether it be chilled, creamy, rich, exotic, spicy, fruity, hearty or lavish! If *Carrot and Coriander Soup* and *Tamatar ka Shorba* are palate soothers then there are some stomach fillers such as *Southern Italian Soup* and the *Lemon and Tortilla Soup*! Soup is an international star. So, be it dinnertime in Italy or a midday meal in a Chinese home, a soup bowl is to be on the table!

An old Spanish saying enlightened the diner by stating: "If given to choose between soup and love, then choose the former". Truly with all the goodness packed into that bowl, it is definitely comforting and soothing food. Since studies have shown that regular consumption of fruits and vegetables is associated with a reduced risk for chronic degenerative diseases why not include it in the form of soups? You will find the truth in a sip of the *Broccoli and Toasted Almond Soup* and the *Vegetable Clear Soup*.

The daily rut needs some perky additions that will be new in taste, texture and tang! Even if one riffles through old recipe books one would find superb recipes of salads. I am sure salads are something that are fun to eat and make, don't you agree? When it comes to stomach fillers, salads are a sure hit! They are also nutritious as the calorie count in most is acceptable! A tossed salad provides a platform for seasonal vegetables to show off their best performance. We have great stars performing in the *Pineapple Waldorf* and the *Tabbouleh*. Or then let us enjoy Indian delights such as *chaats* that are not only mouth watering but also nutritious. Wonderful examples are the *Moong Mauth Chaat* and the *Fruit Chaat*.

My suggestion is that you combine a good hearty soup with a delicious tossed salad and make a meal of it. You will not only feel light but will feel right also. All recipes serve four and form part of a menu. Start off with a soup and a good salad and the rest will follow....

CONTENTS

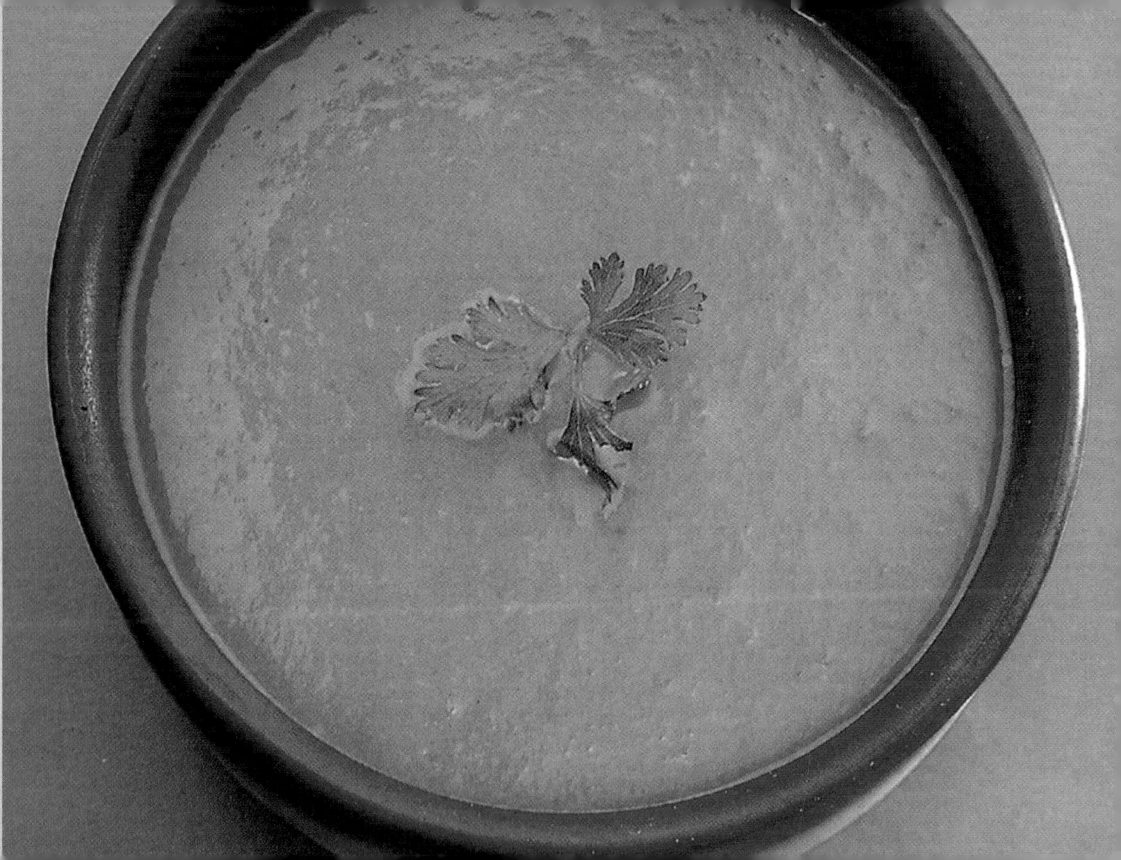

Carrot and Coriander Soup

CARROT AND CORIANDER SOUP

INGREDIENTS

Carrots .... 7-8 medium sized
Onion .... 1 medium sized
Garlic .... 6-8 cloves
Fresh coriander leaves ..... 1 medium bunch
Butter .... 2 tbsps

Bay leaves 2
Peppercorns 8-10
White pepper powder .... ½ tsp
Salt .... to taste

METHOD OF PREPARATION

1 Peel, wash and roughly chop carrots. Peel, wash and chop onion and garlic. Clean, wash and chop coriander leaves finely. Reserve stems.

2 Heat butter in a pan, add bay leaves, peppercorns, onion and garlic and fry for two minutes.

3 Add carrots, coriander stems and five cups of water and bring to a

boil. Cook till carrots are completely cooked. Let cool. Remove carrots and blend into a smooth puree.

4 Reduce stock slightly by boiling on high heat and strain.

5 Pour puree in a pan and slowly add strained stock to reach the desired consistency. Bring to a boil again. Add white pepper powder dissolved in a little water. Add salt to taste. Stir in finely chopped fresh coriander leaves.

6 Serve piping hot.

TAMATAR KA SHORBA

INGREDIENTS

Tomatoes .... 10 medium sized
Ginger .... 1 inch piece
Garlic .... 4 cloves
Red chillies (fresh) 4
Curry leaves 8
Coriander seeds .... 2 tsps

Turmeric powder .... ½ tsp
Salt .... to taste
Oil .... 1 tbsp
Cumin seeds .... ½ tsp
Mustard seeds .... ½ tsp

METHOD OF PREPARATION

1   Wash and halve tomatoes. Peel, wash and chop ginger and garlic.
    Remove stems, wash and chop fresh red chillies. Wash and pat dry
    curry leaves. Roast coriander seeds.
2   Take four and a half cups of water in a deep pan, add tomatoes,
    ginger, coriander seeds, turmeric powder and half of the curry leaves
    and bring to a boil. Lower heat and simmer for half an hour. Strain.
3   Reheat the liquid, add salt to taste and simmer for fifteen minutes.
4   Heat oil in a pan, add cumin seeds and mustard seeds. When they
    crackle add garlic, fresh red chillies and remaining curry leaves.
5   Sauté for a minute and add to the simmering *shorba*. Stir well and
    serve hot.

23

CHILLED MUST!
MELON SOUP

INGREDIENTS

Musk melon.... 1 (approx. 1 kg.)
Ginger .... 1 inch piece
Fresh mint leaves ..... a few sprigs
Skimmed milk yogurt .... ¼ cup

Lemon juice .... 3 tbsps
Crushed ice .... 2 cups
Salt .... to taste
Pepper powder .... ¼ tsp

CHEF'S TIP

1. Consistency of this soup is normally very thick, however if you prefer you may thin it down by adding a half a cup of chilled skimmed milk.

2. Go easy on mint leaves as too much mint flavour and taste can be too over powering.

METHOD OF PREPARATION

1 Cut musk melon into two, remove and discard seeds. Peel and cut into one inch sized pieces.
2 Peel, wash and roughly chop ginger. Clean and wash mint leaves thoroughly. Reserve a sprig for garnish.
3 In a blender or a food processor, puree musk melon along with ginger and mint leaves. Add yogurt, lemon juice and crushed ice, blend for a few minutes more.
4 Season with salt and pepper powder.
5 Serve chilled garnished with a sprig of mint.

SWEET CORN VEGETABLE SOUP

INGREDIENTS

Sweet corn (cream style)150 gms
Sweet corn kernels .... ½ cup
Carrot .... ¼ medium sized
Cabbage .... ¼ small sized
Spring onion greens 1
Cornstarch .... 3 tbsps

Oil .... 2 tbsps
Vegetable stock .... 4-5 cups
Salt .... to taste
White pepper powder .... ¼ tsp
Sugar .... ½ tbsp
Ajinomoto .... ¼ tsp

METHOD OF PREPARATION

1 Peel, wash and chop carrot into small pieces. Wash, trim, remove core and finely chop cabbage. Wash, trim and chop spring onion greens.

2 Blend cornstarch in half a cup of water and keep aside.

3 Heat oil in a wok or a pan and add cabbage, carrot and corn kernels. Stir-fry for two minutes. Stir in vegetable stock and bring to a boil.

4   Mix in cream style sweet corn and continue cooking for two to three minutes or until the cream style corn is mixed well.

5   Add salt, white pepper powder, sugar and Ajinomoto. Stir in blended cornstarch, cook on high heat for a minute or until the soup has thickened, stirring continuously.

6   Serve piping hot, garnished with chopped spring onion greens.

CELESTIAL VEGETABLE SOUP

INGREDIENTS

Fresh button mushrooms 8-10
Carrot .... 1 medium sized
Capsicum .... 1 medium sized
Green peas (shelled) .... ½ cup
Vegetable stock .... 3 cups
Cornstarch .... 2 tbsps

Oil .... 1 tsp
Sweet corn niblets .... 2 tbsps
Salt .... to taste
Sugar .... a pinch
Red chillies whole (crushed) .. ½ tsp

METHOD OF PREPARATION

1   Clean, wash and cut mushrooms into four. Peel, wash and cut carrot into one-fourth inch sized pieces. Wash capsicum, halve, deseed and cut into one-fourth inch sized pieces. Wash and drain green peas.

2   Boil carrot and green peas in vegetable stock or water. Keep aside. Dissolve cornstarch in half a cup of water.

3   Heat oil, add capsicum and mushrooms and cook for two to three minutes on high heat.

4   Add warm vegetable stock or water along with carrot, green peas and sweet corn niblets. Bring to a boil. Add salt to taste, sugar and crushed red chillies.

5   Add blended cornstarch, stirring continuously. Cook on high heat for one minute. Serve piping hot.

Celestial Vegetable Soup

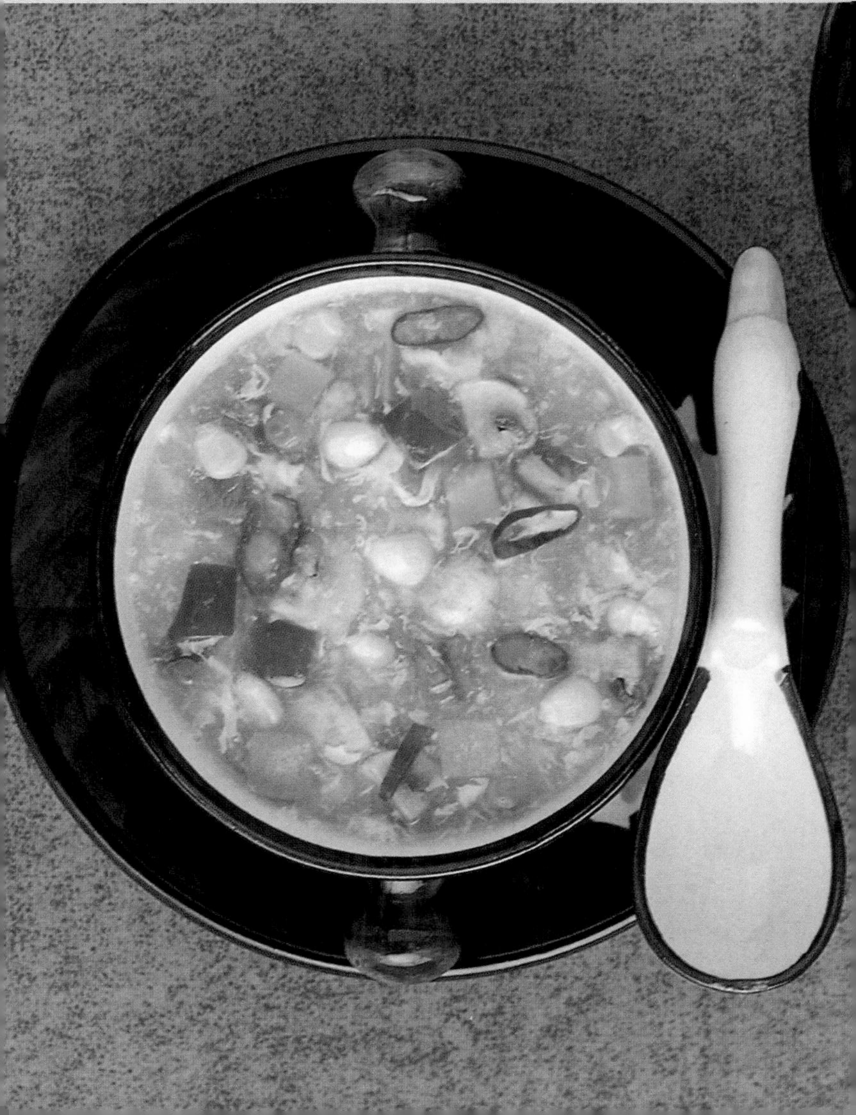

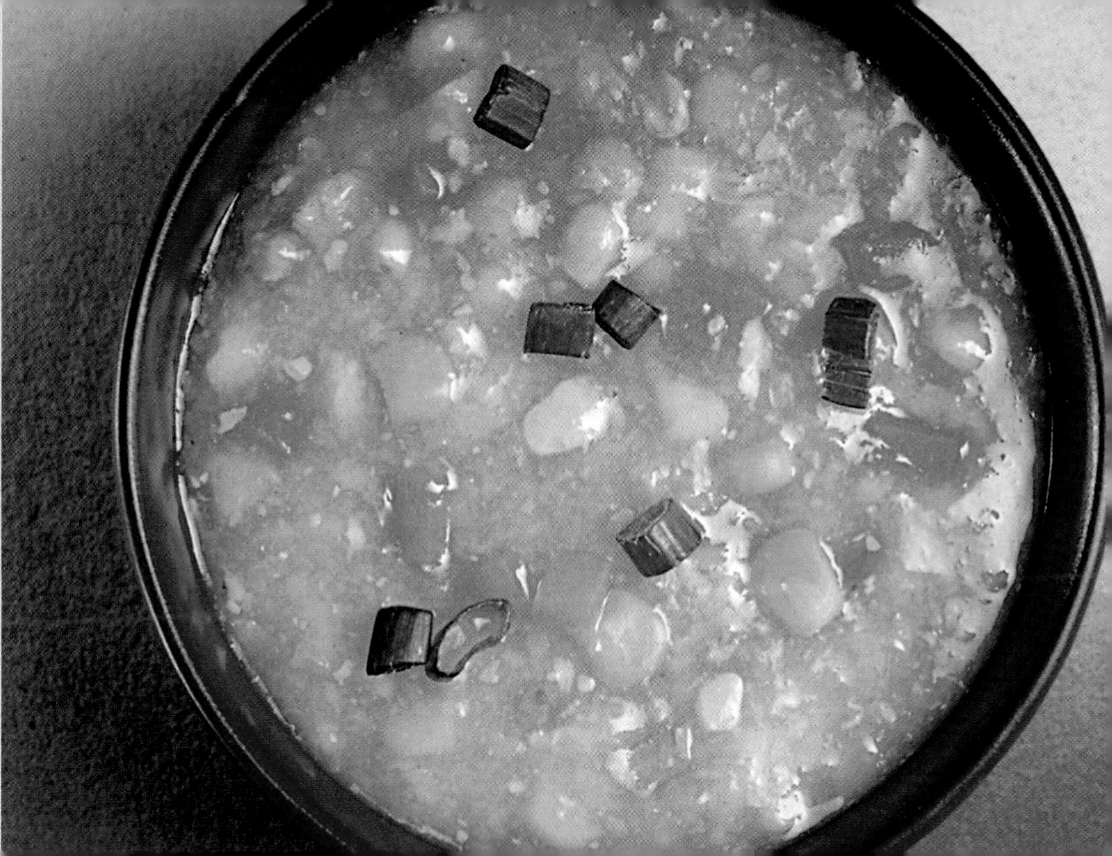

Sweetcorn Vegetable Soup

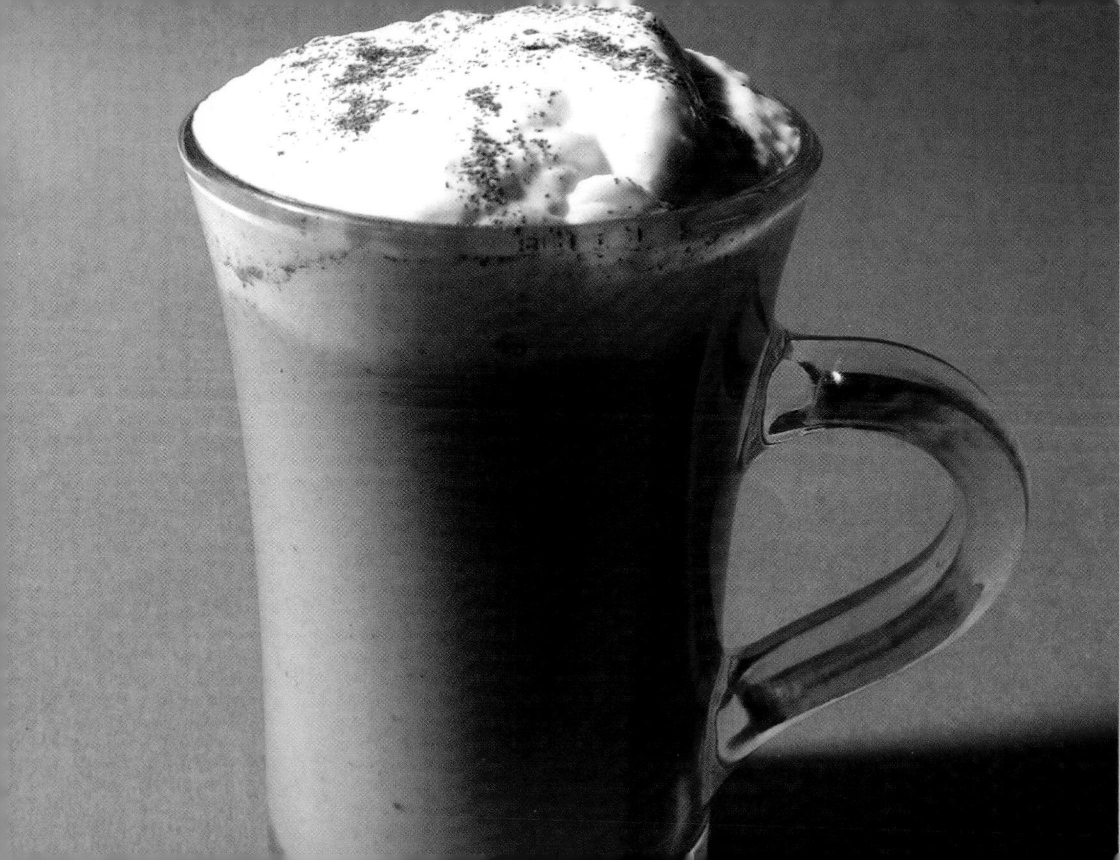

Mushroom Cappuccino

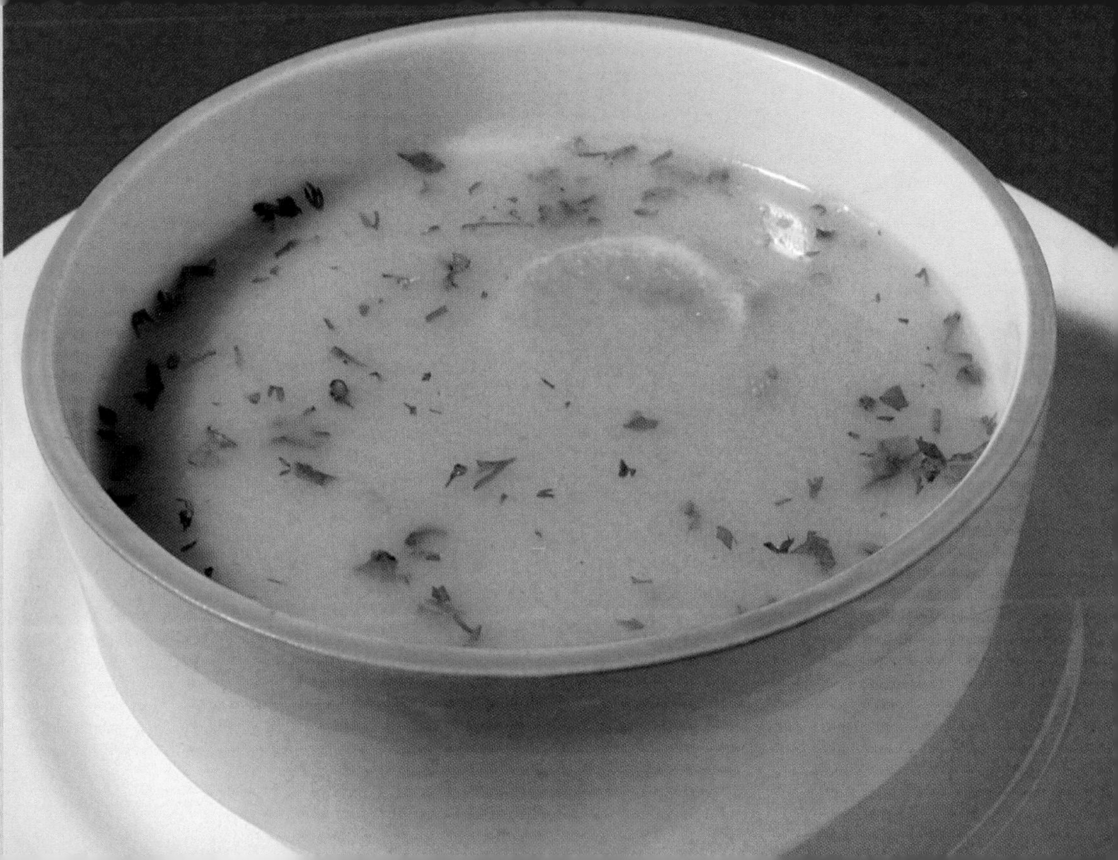

Lemon and Coriander Soup

LEMON AND CORIANDER SOUP

INGREDIENTS

Lemon juice .... 2 tbsps
Fresh coriander leaves .... 1 small bunch
Cabbage .... ¼ small sized
Carrot .... 1 medium sized
Onion .... 1 medium sized
Spring onion bulb .. 1 medium sized
Ginger .... 1 inch piece

Garlic .... 5 cloves
Peppercorns 7-8
Oil .... 2 tbsps
Gram flour (*besan*) .... 2 tbsps
Vegetable stock (or water) .... 2½ cups
Salt .... to taste

METHOD OF PREPARATION

1   Clean, wash coriander leaves and reserve the stems. Wash and finely chop coriander leaves. Trim, wash, remove core of cabbage and cut into half centimeter sized cubes. Peel, wash and cut carrot into half centimeter sized cubes.

2   Peel, wash and chop onion, spring onion bulb, ginger and garlic. Crush peppercorns.

3   Heat oil in a pan. Add onion, spring onion bulb, ginger and garlic and sauté till translucent. Add gram flour and continue to sauté till you get a nice aroma.

4   Add vegetable stock, coriander stems and bring to a boil. Add crushed peppercorns and continue to boil.

5   Add half of the chopped coriander leaves and cook for five to ten minutes. Strain and keep aside cooked vegetables.

6   Heat the strained soup. Add salt, lemon juice and bring to a boil again.

7   Season with the remaining chopped coriander leaves and serve hot.

Note: To make vegetable stock cook together one medium sized sliced onion, half a medium sized sliced carrot, two inch chopped celery stalk, two cloves of crushed garlic with five cups of water, one bay leaf, five to six peppercorns and two to three cloves for about fifteen minutes. Strain, cool and store in a refrigerator to use when required.

MUSHROOM CAPPUCCINO

INGREDIENTS

Mushrooms .... 15 large sized
Onion .... 1 small sized
Garlic .... 4-6 cloves
Butter .... 1 tbsp
Bay leaf..1
Vegetable stock................ 4 cups

Salt .... to taste
White pepper powder .... ¼ tsp
Fresh cream .... ¾ cup
Milk (chilled) .... 2 cups
Cinnamon powder .... 1 tsp

METHOD OF PREPARATION

1   Clean, wash and thickly slice mushrooms. Peel, wash and finely chop onion and garlic.

2   Melt butter in a heavy bottomed pan, add bay leaf, onion and garlic and sauté for two to three minutes or till onion becomes translucent.

3   Add mushrooms and sauté for a minute. Add one cup of vegetable

stock and cook for five more minutes. Remove from heat and cool. Remove bay leaf.

4 Make puree of the cooked mushrooms. Add remaining vegetable stock to it.

5 Return to heat and bring to a boil, add salt and white pepper powder and simmer the soup for two to three minutes.

6 Add cream and remove from heat. Place soup in individual cups.

7 In a chilled bowl take the chilled milk and beat it with a fork. This will develop froth in it which can be collected with a ladle and placed on the hot mushroom soup giving it a cappuccino effect. Sprinkle cinnamon powder and serve.

CHEF'S TIP

Milk with high fat content will give best results with the froth making.

LEMON AND
TORTILLA SOUP

INGREDIENTS

Corn tortillas	2	Walnuts	4
Tomato	1 medium sized	Oil	2 tsps + to deep fry
Onions	2 medium sized	Vegetable stock	4 cups
Green chillies	4	Salt	to taste
Lemon	1	Lemon juice	1 tbsp
Saffron	a pinch	Fresh cream	½ cup

METHOD OF PREPARATION

1　Cut tortillas into five by one centimeter strips. Wash and chop tomato. Peel, wash and chop onions. Remove stems, wash and chop green chillies. Wash and cut lemon into four. Dissolve saffron in a few drops of warm water. Shell walnuts and cut into four.

2　Heat sufficient oil in a deep frying pan and fry tortilla strips until brown and crisp. Drain onto an absorbent paper and keep aside.

3   Heat two teaspoons of oil in a large saucepan, add onions, green chillies and sauté till onions are soft.
4   Add vegetable stock and salt. Cover and simmer for twenty minutes.
5   Add tomato and simmer for another five minutes. Stir in lemon juice, walnut pieces and saffron. Remove soup from heat.
6   Add fried tortilla strips and fresh cream. Garnish with lemon pieces and serve hot.

VEGETABLE MANCHOW SOUP

INGREDIENTS

Chinese mushrooms (dried) . 2-3
Fresh button mushrooms 2-3
Cabbage .... ¼ small sized
Tofu (bean curd) .... 50 gms
Capsicum .... 1 medium sized
Green chillies 2
Bamboo shoots .... 2 slices
Carrot .... 1 medium sized
Ginger .... ½ inch piece
Garlic .... 2-3 cloves
Spring onion 1

Noodles .... 1 cup
Oil .... 2 tbsps + to deep fry
Cornstarch .... 3 tbsps
Red chilli sauce .... ½ tbsp
Soy sauce .... 2 tbsps
White pepper powder .... ½ tsp
Ajinomoto .... ¼ tsp
Salt .... to taste
Vegetable stock .... 4-5 cups
Vinegar .... 1 tbsp

METHOD OF PREPARATION

1 Wash and soak Chinese mushrooms in hot water for fifteen minutes. Drain, wash thoroughly and finely chop.
2 Wash and finely chop mushrooms, cabbage and tofu. Wash, halve, deseed and finely chop capsicum. Remove stems, wash and finely chop green chillies.
3 Boil the bamboo shoot slices in one cup of water for three to four minutes. Drain completely, cool and chop finely.
4 Peel, wash and finely chop carrot, ginger and garlic. Trim, wash and finely chop spring onion and reserve some chopped spring onion greens for garnish.
5 Blanch noodles in hot water, remove and drain well. Heat sufficient oil in a wok and deep-fry the boiled noodles for two to three minutes or until light brown and crisp. Remove and drain onto an absorbent kitchen towel. Blend cornstarch in half a cup of water and keep aside.
6 Heat two tablespoons of oil in a pan, add ginger, garlic, green chillies and stir-fry briefly. Add spring onion and cook for a couple of minutes.

7 Add mushrooms, cabbage, bamboo shoot, tofu, capsicum, carrot and cook on medium heat, stirring continuously for two minutes.

8 Add chilli sauce, soy sauce, pepper powder, Ajinomoto, salt to taste and stir well to mix. Stir in the vegetable stock and bring to a boil. Reduce heat and simmer for two to three minutes.

9 Stir in blended cornstarch and cook for two minutes or until soup thickens, stirring continuously.

10 Stir in vinegar and serve piping hot, garnished with crispy fried noodles and spring onion greens.

BROCCOLI AND TOASTED ALMOND SOUP

INGREDIENTS

Broccoli	400 gms	Almonds	10-12
Onion	1 medium sized	Low fat milk	1 cup
Garlic	4 cloves	Salt	to taste
Celery	2 inch stalk	White pepper powder	to taste

METHOD OF PREPARATION

1   Cut broccoli into small florets and wash well. Soak in salted water for ten to fifteen minutes and drain.

2   Peel, wash and roughly chop onion and garlic. Trim, wash and chop celery stalk.

3   Broil or dry roast almonds on medium heat till almond skin changes

its colour slightly. Remove from heat, cool and slice into slivers.

4 Heat four cups of vegetable stock or water with onion, garlic and celery. Bring it to a boil.

5 Add broccoli florets and cover pan. Continue to cook for five to seven minutes or till broccoli is just done.

6 Remove from heat, cool and puree in a blender.

7 Add milk to pureed broccoli and mix well. Bring to a boil again.

8 Add salt and white pepper powder to taste. Stir in toasted almond slivers and serve hot.

FRENCH ONION & GARLIC SOUP

INGREDIENTS

Onions .... 3 medium sized	Cheese .... (grated) ¼ cup
Garlic .... 5-6 cloves	Oil .... 1 tbsp
Carrot .... 1 medium sized	Vegetable stock .... 4 cups
Brown bread .... 4 slices	Salt .... to taste
Olive oil .... 1 tbsp	White pepper powder .... ¼ tsp

METHOD OF PREPARATION

1 Peel, wash and slice onions. Peel, wash and chop half of the garlic.
2 Peel, wash and cut carrot into two lengthwise. Cut into thin slices.
3 Cut brown bread into small roundels, toast with olive oil and rub with remaining garlic cloves.
4 Heat oil in a thick-bottomed pan and sauté onions till brown. Keep aside a few slices of fried onions for garnishing. Add chopped garlic and sauté.
5 Add carrots and sauté for two to three minutes.

6   Add vegetable stock and bring to a boil. Reduce heat and let it simmer for ten to fifteen minutes. Add salt and white pepper powder.

7   To serve, ladle soup into individual bowls and float the toasted brown bread, top it with grated cheese and reserved fried onions and serve hot.

CHEF'S TIP

Since the quantity of oil used for frying onions is minimal, sliced onions would not become crisp as in the case of traditional French Onion Soup. However, if available, use dehydrated sliced onions. They keep crisp.

MINESTRONE

INGREDIENTS

Carrot .... 1 medium sized	Fresh basil leaves 10-12
Potato .... 1 medium sized	Tomatoes .... 4 medium sized
Zucchini .... 1 medium sized	Oil .... 1½ tbsps
Garlic .... 4-6 cloves	Vegetable stock .... 4 cups
Onion .... 1 medium sized	Macaroni .... 2 tbsps
Green peas (shelled) .... ¼ cup	Salt .... to taste
Celery .... 1 inch stalk	White pepper powder .... ½ tsp
Leek .... ½ stalk	Parmesan cheese (optional, grated)
French beans 3-4	.... ½ cup

METHOD OF PREPARATION

1   Peel, wash and cut carrot, potato and zucchini into one centimeter sized cubes. Peel, wash and chop garlic and onion. Wash and drain green peas.

2 Trim, wash and cut celery and leek to one centimeter sized pieces. String, wash and cut French beans into one centimeter sized pieces. Wash and cut half of the basil leaves into strips and keep in cold water.

3 Wash tomatoes, cut the base and give a cross cut with a sharp knife on the top, just superficially. Boil some water in a pan, put tomatoes in it for ten to twenty seconds and transfer immediately into a bowl of cold water. Peel the skin with hand, cut into halves, remove seeds and cut into one centimeter sized pieces.

4 Heat oil (preferably olive oil) in a pan, add garlic, onion and carrot and sauté till onions are translucent. Add leek and celery and stir-fry for a minute.

5 Add French beans, zucchini, potatoes, green peas and tomatoes. Add remaining half of the fresh basil leaves broken by hand. Sauté for a couple of minutes and add vegetable stock and bring to a boil.

6 Add macaroni and boil on high heat for five to seven minutes. Season with salt and white pepper powder.
7 Serve hot, garnished with fresh basil strips and grated Parmesan cheese.

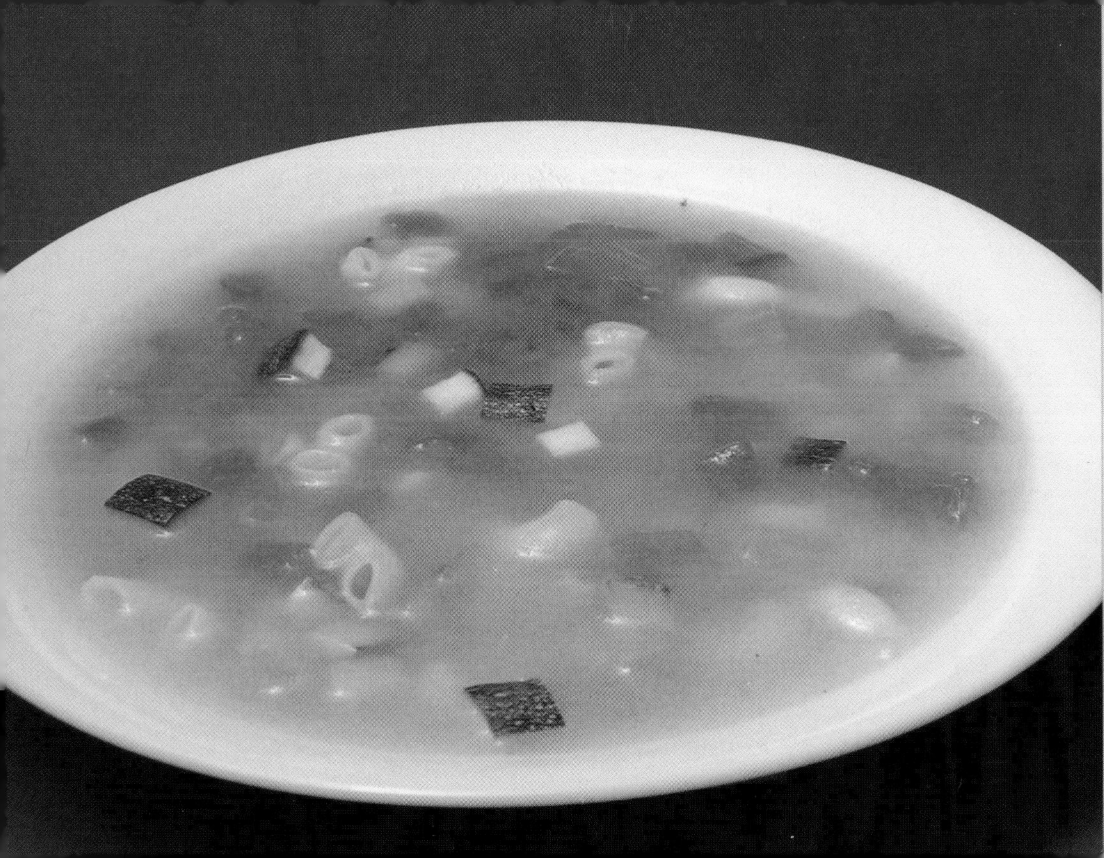

Minestrone

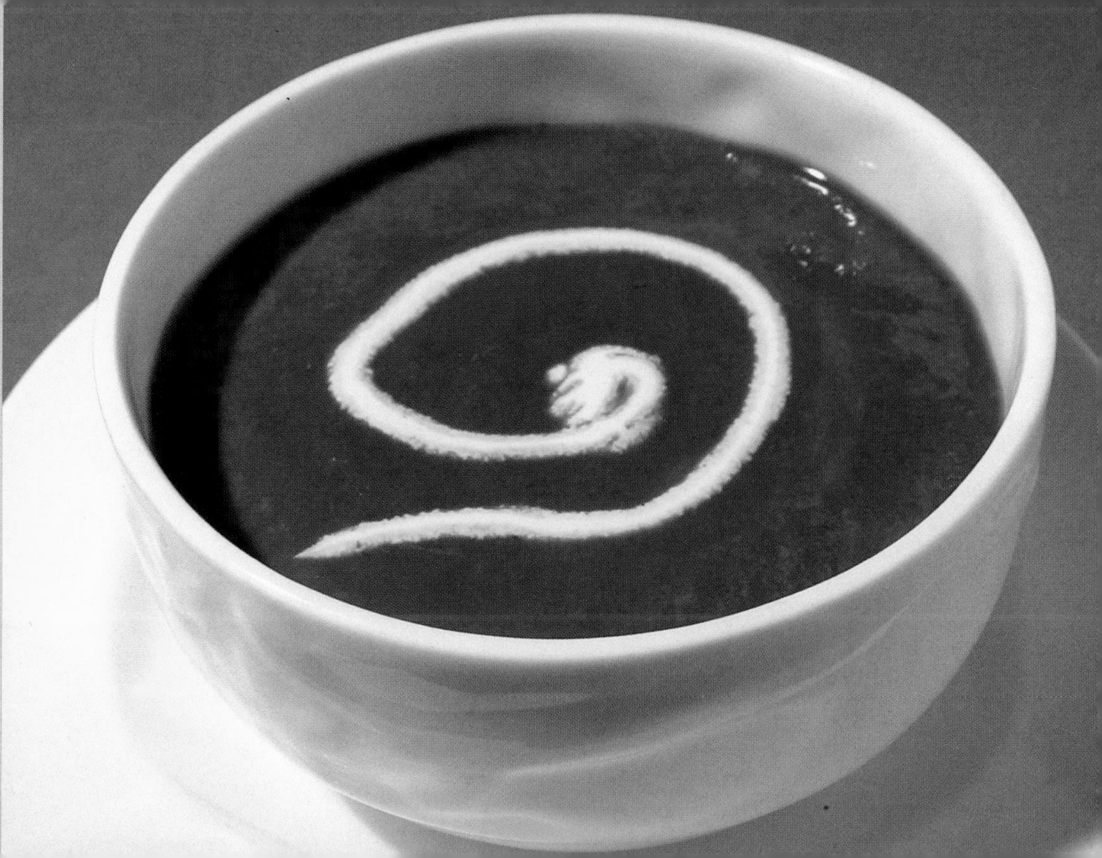

Palak Shorba

PALAK SHORBA

INGREDIENTS

Spinach (*palak*) ... 2 medium bunches	Cinnamon .... 1 inch stick
Ginger .... 3 one inch pieces	Refined flour (*maida*) ...... 2 tbsps
Garlic .... 5 cloves	Peppercorns 4-5
Onion .... 1 medium sized	Bay leaves 4
Butter .... 2 tbsps	Salt .... to taste
Black cardamoms 3	White pepper powder .... ¼ tsp
Cloves 2	Roasted cumin powder .... 1 tsp

METHOD OF PREPARATION

1   Clean and wash spinach leaves thoroughly under running water. Blanch the leaves in five to six cups of boiling hot water for two to three minutes. Drain, refresh in cold water and puree them in a mixer.
2   Peel, wash and finely chop ginger, garlic and onion.
3   Heat butter in a deep pan. Add black cardamoms, cloves, cinnamon, refined flour and sauté for two to three minutes.

4 Add ginger, garlic, onion and continue to sauté for about five minutes.

5 Add peppercorns, bay leaves, salt, white pepper powder, roasted cumin powder and five cups of water. Stir and simmer for ten minutes stirring at intervals.

6 Strain the stock. Add spinach puree to the strained stock and mix well.

7 Cook for four to five minutes. Serve piping hot.

PEPPER RASAM

INGREDIENTS

Pigeon peas split (*toovar dal*) ... 3 tbsps
Garlic .... 3 cloves
Curry leaves 20
Peppercorns 10-12
Bengal gram split (*chana dal*) .. 1 tsp
Black gram split (*dhuli urad dal*) .. 1 tsp
Red chillies whole 6-7
Fenugreek seeds .... ¼ tsp
Cumin seeds .... ½ tsp
Mustard seeds .... ¾ tsp
Coriander seeds .... 1 tsp

Oil .... 1 tbsp
Salt .... to taste
Turmeric powder .... ¼ tsp
Tamarind pulp.................. 2 tbsps
Jaggery (grated) .... 1 tbsp
Tempering
Oil .... 1 tbsp
Mustard seeds...................... ½ tsp
Red chillies whole 2
Asafoetida .... ¼ tsp

METHOD OF PREPARATION

1   Wash and soak *toovar dal* in one cup of water for half an hour and

pressure-cook the *dal* in one cup of water. When cooked mash well and keep aside.

2 Peel, wash and crush garlic. Wash and pat dry curry leaves. Coarsely powder peppercorns.

3 Dry roast and powder the *chana dal*, *urad dal*, red chillies, fenugreek seeds, cumin seeds, half a teaspoon of mustard seeds and coriander seeds.

4 Heat oil in a *kadai* and add garlic, remaining mustard seeds, crushed peppercorns and ten curry leaves.

5 When the mustard starts to splutter, add mashed *dal*, the *masala* powder mixed with a little water, salt, turmeric powder, tamarind pulp and jaggery. Blend well and add five cups of water. Bring to a boil.

6 Simmer on low heat for ten to fifteen minutes. Strain it through a muslin cloth.

7 Heat oil in a pan for tempering. Add mustard seeds, allow them to crackle, add red chillies, asafoetida and the remaining curry leaves. Pour over the *rasam*. Serve hot.

SOUTHERN ITALIAN VEGETABLE SOUP

INGREDIENTS

Carrot .... 1 medium sized
Potatoes .... 2 medium sized
Cabbage .... ¼ small sized
Tomatoes .... 2 medium sized
Onion .... 1 medium sized
Garlic .... 4 cloves
Celery .... 1 inch stalk

Fresh basil .... 6-8 leaves
Olive oil .... 1 tsp
Salt .... to taste
White pepper powder .... to taste
Macaroni .... ¼ cup
Vegetable stock .... 4 cups

METHOD OF PREPARATION

1   Peel, wash and chop carrot into very small dices. Peel, wash and
    cut potato into very small dices and leave them in water. Wash,
    remove core and cut cabbage also into very small dices.

2   Wash, remove eyes of tomatoes and make a small incision at the

bottom of each. Boil two cups of water and blanch tomatoes for two minutes and remove immediately. Peel, deseed and puree or mince tomatoes.

3 Peel, wash and finely chop onion and garlic. Trim, wash and chop celery and basil leaves, reserving a few for garnish.

4 Heat olive oil in a pan, add onion and garlic and sauté till they turn translucent.

5 Add celery, carrot and potato pieces. Stir continuously and cook for five minutes.

6 Add cabbage, tomatoes and cook stirring continuously. Add salt, pepper, basil and macaroni, stir and add stock and bring it to a boil.

7 Reduce heat and simmer till vegetables are cooked and the soup has thickened.

8 Crush remaining basil with a pestle and garnish the soup.

MATAR KA SHORBA

INGREDIENTS

Green peas...................... 500 gms	*Ghee* or oil .... 3 tbsps
Onion .... 1 medium sized	Cumin seeds .... ½ tsp
Ginger .... 2 one inch pieces	Bay leaves 2
Garlic .... 8-10 cloves	Salt .... to taste
Green chillies 2	Fresh cream .... ¼ cup

METHOD OF PREPARATION

1 Shell, wash and boil green peas in two cups of water. Blend in a blender to make a smooth puree.
2 Peel, wash and finely chop onion. Peel, wash ginger and garlic. Remove stems and wash green chillies. Grind ginger, garlic with green chillies to make a paste.
3 Heat *ghee* or oil in a pan, add cumin seeds and bay leaves, stir-fry for half a minute. Add onion and sauté till it turns a light pink. Add ginger-garlic-green chilli paste. Sauté for one to two minutes.

4   Add green peas puree. Cook for five minutes, stirring continuously. Add three cups of water and bring to a boil.
5   Season with salt and stir. Remove bay leaves and discard. Reduce heat and cook further for five minutes. This soup is of thick consistency, however you may make it of the consistency of your liking, by varying the quantity of water used.
6   Stir in fresh cream and serve hot garnished with a swirl of cream.

Matar Ka Shorba

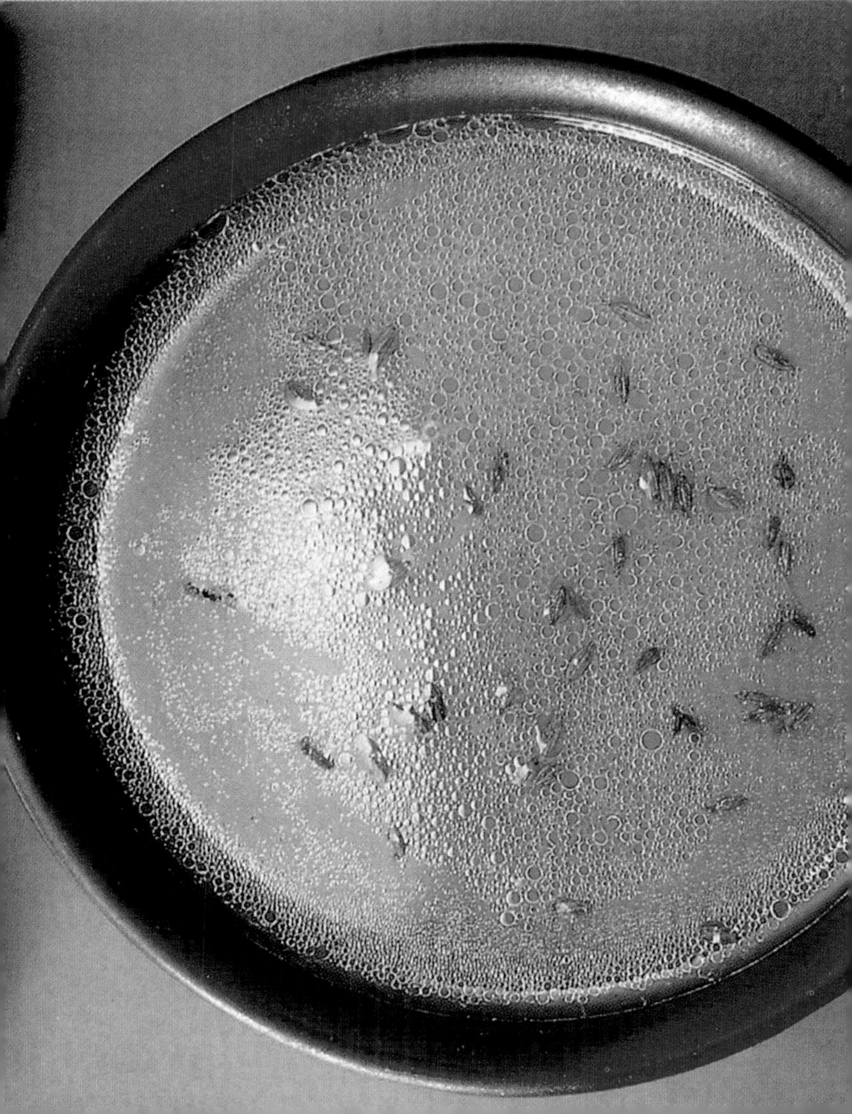

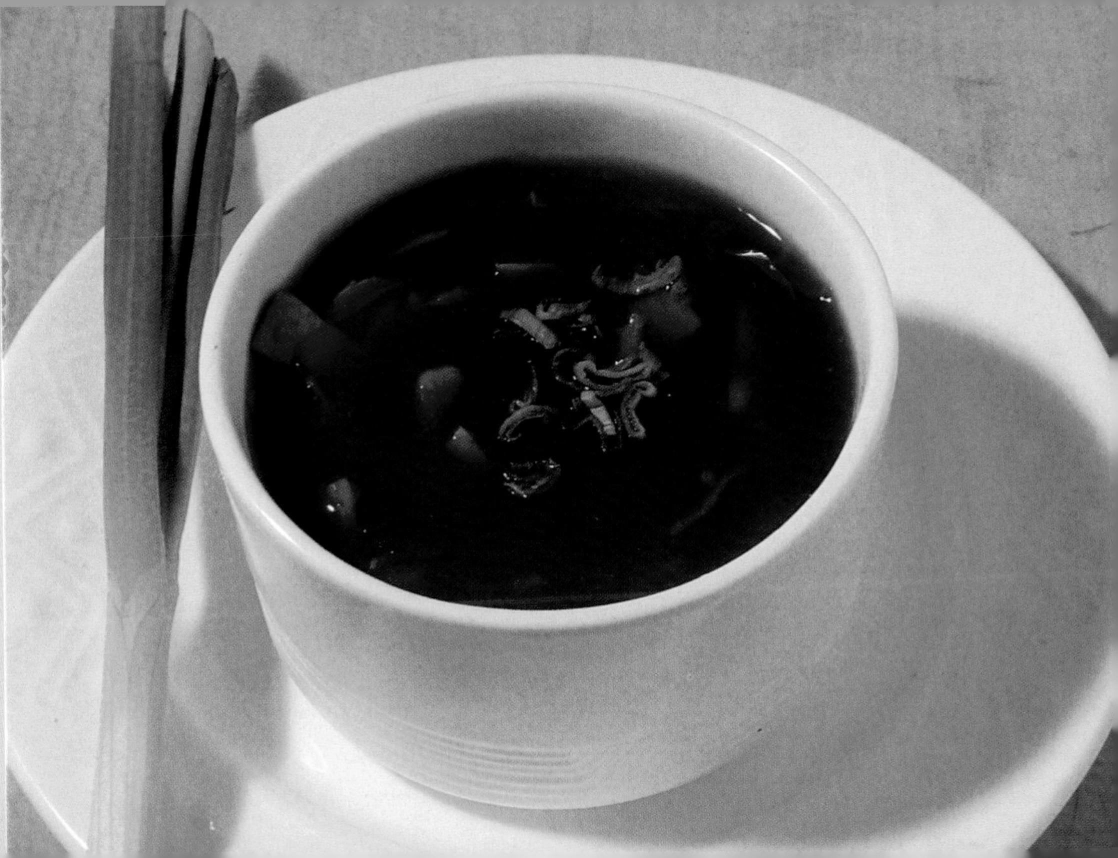

Hot and Sour Vegetable Soup

HOT AND SOUR VEGETABLE SOUP

INGREDIENTS

Onion .... 1 small sized
Garlic .... 2-3 cloves
Carrot .... ½ medium sized
Ginger .... 1 inch piece
Cabbage .... ¼ small sized
Celery .... 2 inch stalk
Fresh button mushrooms 2
Spring onion greens 1
Bamboo shoot .... 1 slice
Capsicum .... ½ medium sized
French beans 4-6

Cornstarch .... 3 tbsps
Oil .... 2 tbsps
White pepper powder .... ½ tsp
Salt .... to taste
Sugar .... ½ tsp
Ajinomoto .... ¼ tsp
Soy sauce .... 2 tbsps
Green chilli sauce .... 2 tbsps
Vegetable stock .... 4-5 cups
Vinegar .... 2 tbsps
Chilli oil .... 1 tbsp

METHOD OF PREPARATION

1 Peel, wash and finely chop onion and garlic. Wash, peel, grate carrot and ginger. Wash, trim and finely chop cabbage, celery and mushrooms. Trim, wash and chop spring onion greens and keep aside.

2 Boil the bamboo shoot slice in sufficient water for two to three minutes, drain, cool and finely chop.

3 Wash, deseed and finely chop capsicum. String, wash and finely chop French beans. Blend cornstarch in half a cup of water.

4 Heat oil in a wok or a saucepan, add onion, ginger, garlic and stir-fry briefly. Add celery, carrot, cabbage, bamboo shoot, mushrooms, capsicum and French beans.

5 Cook for two to three minutes or until vegetables are almost cooked, stirring continuously. Add white pepper powder, salt to taste, sugar, Ajinomoto, soy sauce, green chilli sauce and mix well.

6 Stir in vegetable stock and bring to a boil. Stir in blended cornstarch and continue to cook for a minute or till soup thickens.

7 Stir in vinegar, drizzle chilli oil and serve piping hot, garnished with chopped spring onion greens.

CHEF'S TIP

We have used tinned bamboo shoot slices, which are preserved in brine, hence they have to be boiled in water before use.

WONTON SOUP

INGREDIENTS

Wonton wrappers 16
Cabbage leaves 4-5
Capsicum .... ½ medium sized
French beans 2-3
Carrot .... ½ medium sized
Spring onion 1
Garlic .... 2 cloves

Oil .... ½ tbsp
White pepper powder .... ¼ tsp
Salt .... to taste
Soy sauce .... 1 tsp
Vegetable stock .... 5-6 cups
Ajinomoto .... ¼ tsp

METHOD OF PREPARATION

1 Wash, trim and finely chop cabbage leaves. Wash, deseed and finely chop capsicum. String, wash and finely chop French beans. Peel, wash and finely chop carrot.

2 Wash, trim, finely chop spring onion and reserve some chopped greens for garnish. Peel, wash and finely chop garlic.

3 Heat oil in a wok, add chopped garlic and stir-fry briefly. Add

chopped spring onion, capsicum, French beans, carrot, cabbage and continue to cook for a couple of minutes or until the vegetables are cooked, stirring continuously.

4   Add half the quantity of white pepper powder, salt to taste and stir in soy sauce. Cook on high heat for half a minute, remove and cool.

5   Divide the prepared filling into sixteen equal portions. Place a portion of the filling in the centre of each wonton wrapper, wet the edges, fold into half diagonally and twist the ends and stick.

6   Heat stock in a wok or a pan, add the remaining white pepper powder, Ajinomoto, salt to taste and bring to a boil.

7   Reduce heat, gently slide in the prepared wontons and simmer for three to four minutes.

8   Serve piping hot, garnished with reserved chopped spring onion greens.

VEGETABLE CLEAR SOUP

INGREDIENTS

Carrot .... ½ medium sized	Fresh button mushrooms 6-8
Celery .... 1 stalk	Bean sprouts .... ½ cup
Chinese cabbage .... 4-6 leaves	Vegetable stock .... 4-5 cups
Spring onion 1	Ajinomoto .... ¼ tsp
Red capsicum .... 1 medium sized	Peppercorns (crushed) .... ½ tsp
Snow peas 8-10	Salt .... to taste
Garlic .... 2-3 cloves	Lemon juice .... 1 tsp

METHOD OF PREPARATION

1 Peel, wash and cut carrot into two lengthwise. Cut it further into thin slices. Trim, wash and diagonally slice celery.

2 Wash, trim and dice Chinese cabbage into one inch sized pieces. Wash, trim and slice spring onion. Wash, halve, deseed and cut red

capsicum into one inch sized pieces. Wash, string and cut snow paws into two.

3   Peel, wash and crush garlic. Clean, wash and slice mushrooms. Wash and drain bean sprouts.

4   Heat vegetable stock in a wok or a pan, add garlic and bring to a boil. Add mushrooms, carrot, Chinese cabbage, celery, spring onion, red capsicum, snow peas and cook for two to three minutes.

5   Add Ajinomoto, crushed peppercorns, salt to taste and bean sprouts.

6   Stir in lemon juice and serve piping hot.

THAI VEGETABLE
SOUP

INGREDIENTS

Fresh button mushrooms ....
.... 10-12 medium sized
Carrot................ 1 medium sized
Spring onions..............................2
Fresh coriander leaves................
.........................¼ medium bunch
Lettuce leaves 10-12

Lemon grass..... 2 one-inch stalks
Red chillies whole 3
Lemon juice ....1 tbsp
Vegetable stock .... 3 cups
Bean sprouts ....¾ cup
Salt .... to taste
Thin coconut milk .... 1 cup

METHOD OF PREPARATION

1 Clean, wash and slice mushrooms. Peel, wash and cut carrot into
   thin slices. Wash and finely chop spring onions including some of
   the greens. Clean, wash and chop coriander leaves.
2 Wash and shred lettuce leaves. Wash lemon grass stalks. Remove

stems and chop dry red chillies. Soak them in lemon juice.

3   Bring vegetable stock or water to a boil, add carrots and lemon grass. Cover and reduce heat. Simmer for five minutes. Stir in mushrooms, spring onions, bean sprouts, lettuce leaves and salt to taste. Bring to a boil.

4   Add thin coconut milk, reduce heat, do not cover and stir in chopped dried red chillies soaked in lemon juice.

5   Serve piping hot.

CREAMED RED PUMPKIN AND APPLE SOUP

INGREDIENTS

Red pumpkin	250 gms	Vegetable stock	1 ½ cups
Apples	2 large sized	Skimmed milk	1 cup
Onion	1 large sized	Lemon juice	2 tsps
Fresh parsley	a few sprigs	Salt	to taste
Oil	2 tsps	Curry powder	2 tsps
Bay leaves	2	Pepper powder	½ tsp

METHOD OF PREPARATION

1 Peel, wash and grate red pumpkin. Wash, core and roughly chop apples. Peel, wash and roughly chop onion. Clean, wash and chop parsley.

2 Heat oil in a pan, add bay leaves and onion and sauté till translucent.

3 Add pumpkin and apples. Cook on high heat for a couple of minutes stirring continuously.

4 Add three-fourth cup of vegetable stock and cook vegetables till soft.

5 Cool vegetables, discard bay leaves and blend into a puree in a mixer.

6 Heat pureed vegetables and add another three-fourth cup of vegetable stock and milk. Mix well and bring to a boil.

7 Add lemon juice, salt, curry powder and pepper powder.

8 Serve hot garnished with parsley.

CURRIED
CAULIFLOWER SOUP

INGREDIENTS

Cauliflower .... 1 medium sized
Potato .... 1 medium sized
Onion .... 1 medium sized
Garlic .... 4 cloves
Ginger .... ½ inch piece
Fresh coriander leaves ... a few sprigs
Oil .... 1½ tsps
Vegetable stock .... 4 cups

Cumin seeds .... ½ tsp
Mustard seeds .... ¼ tsp
Turmeric powder .... ½ tsp
Coriander powder .... 2 tsps
Skimmed milk yogurt .... 1 cup
Skimmed milk .... ½ cup
Gram flour (besan) .... 2 tsps
Salt .... to taste

METHOD OF PREPARATION

1   Wash and cut cauliflower into small florets and keep it in salted water.

2   Peel, wash and roughly cut potato into small pieces and keep them

in water.

3   Peel, wash and finely chop onion, garlic and ginger. Clean, wash and chop fresh coriander leaves.

4   Heat three fourth teaspoon of oil in a thick-bottomed pan, add onion and sauté for two minutes. Add garlic and ginger and sauté for a further two minutes. Drain and add potato. Drain and add cauliflower florets and cook on high heat for three to four minutes.

5   Stir in two cups of vegetable stock and bring to a boil. Cover and simmer till cauliflower and potato are cooked.

6   Remove from heat and cool mixture. Puree mixture in a blender.

7   Heat remaining oil, add cumin seeds and mustard seeds. When they start to crackle, add cauliflower-potato puree along with remaining vegetable stock. Mix well and let it simmer. Add turmeric powder and coriander powder and mix well.

8   Whisk skimmed yogurt with skimmed milk in a deep bowl. Add gram flour and continue to whisk so that there are no lumps. Stir it into the soup and cook for a three to four minutes.

9   Season with salt.

10 Serve hot garnished with chopped coriander leaves.

CHEF'S TIP

A leftover dish made of potatoes and cauliflower can be pureed and used to make the above soup.

MINTED GREEN PEAS SOUP

INGREDIENTS

Fresh mint leaves 10-12

Green peas (shelled) .... 1 cup

Onion .... 1 small sized

Garlic .... 2-3 cloves

Potato .... 1 small sized

Butter .... 1 tbsp

Vegetable stock .... 3 cups

Milk .... 1 cup

Salt .... to taste

White pepper powder .... ¼ tsp

Fresh cream .... ½ cup

METHOD OF PREPARATION

1 Clean and wash mint leaves. Wash and drain green peas. Peel, wash and finely chop onion and garlic. Peel, wash and slice potato.

2 Heat butter in a pan, add onion and garlic and sauté for half a minute or till onion turns translucent.

3 Add vegetable stock, potato and mint leaves reserving a few leaves

for garnish. Once the liquid starts boiling add green peas. Boil for five to seven minutes, without covering, on high heat.

4   When done remove from heat, cool and strain. Reserve stock for adding later. Puree the peas and other vegetables using a little stock, if required.

5   Mix puree of peas with the required amount of reserved stock and milk and heat it again. Add salt and white pepper powder.

6   Do not overcook. Finish with cream and serve garnished with remaining mint leaves.

TOMATO PARUPPU RASAM

INGREDIENTS

Tomatoes .... 2 medium sized
Pigeon pea split (*toovar dal*) . 4 tbsps
Fresh coriander leaves ....
.... ¼ medium bunch
Curry leaves 10-12
Tamarind .... ½ lemon sized ball

Red chillies whole 2
Rasam powder .... 1½ tsps
Asafoetida .... ¼ tsp
Salt .... to taste
Pure *ghee* .... 4 tbsps
Mustard seeds .... ½ tsp

METHOD OF PREPARATION

1 Wash and chop tomatoes.
2 Wash, drain and cook *toovar dal* in two cups of water until soft. Strain, mash *dal* well. Reserve the strained cooking liquor.
3 Clean, wash and finely chop coriander leaves. Reserve two tablespoons for garnish. Wash and pat dry curry leaves.

4   Soak tamarind in one cup of warm water, remove pulp and strain. Remove stems and break red chillies into two.

5   Mix tamarind pulp with chopped coriander leaves, *rasam* powder, asafoetida, salt and half the curry leaves and bring to a boil. Reduce heat and simmer for two to three minutes.

6   Add tomatoes and reserved cooking liquor. Simmer for four to five minutes and add mashed *dal*. Stir well and cook for a minute.

7   Remove from heat and sprinkle reserved coriander leaves.

8   Heat pure *ghee* in a tempering pan, add mustard seeds. When they crackle, add broken red chillies and remaining curry leaves. Pour tempering over prepared *rasam* and cover immediately to trap the aroma. Serve hot.

CHEF'S TIP

You can strain this *rasam* and serve in small tumblers with lemon wedges, as an appetizer. Traditionally all *rasams* are made in a vessel made from a special alloy. This gives a unique flavour to the preparation.

Tomato Paruppu Rasam

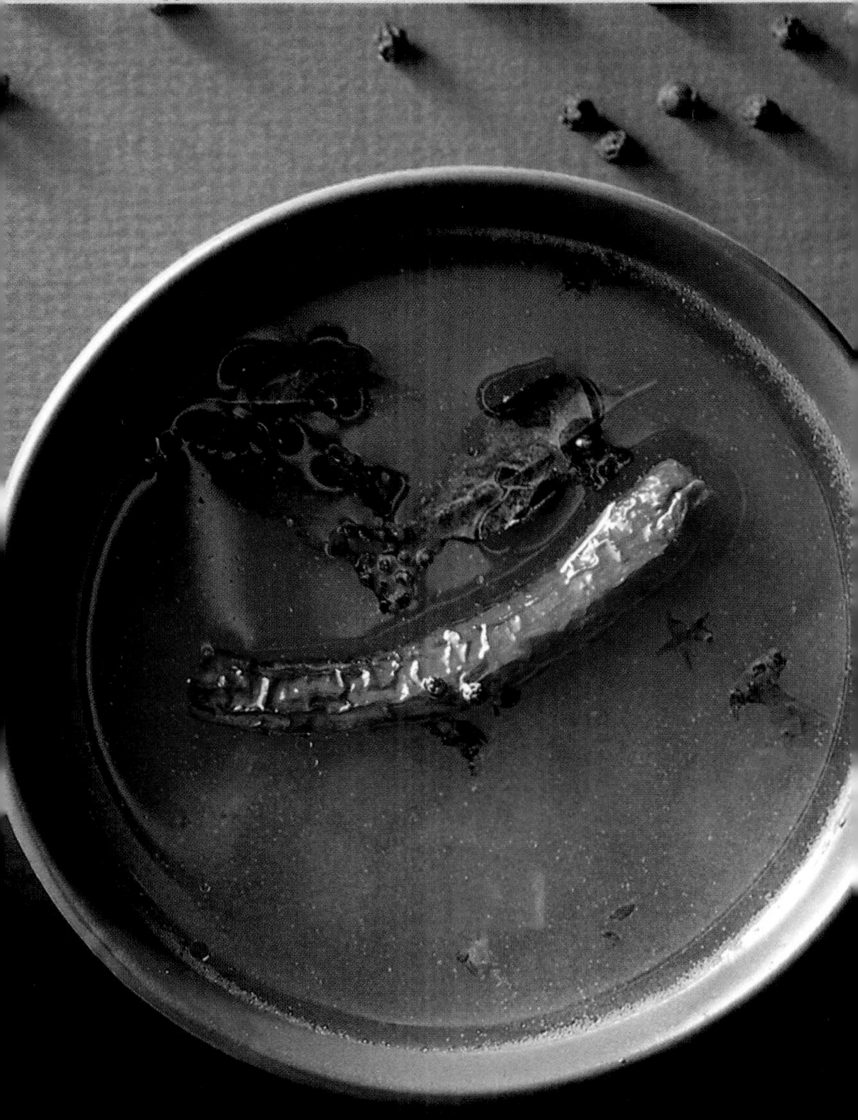

Minted Green Peas Soup

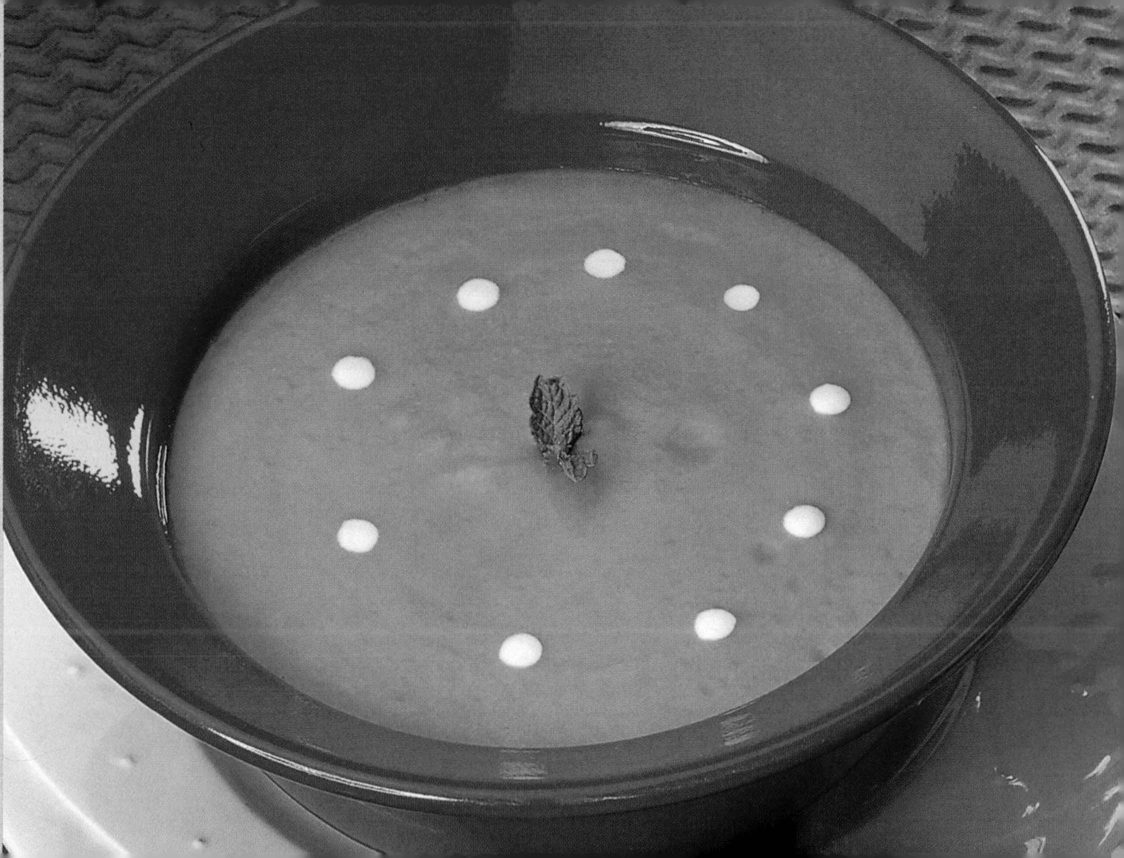

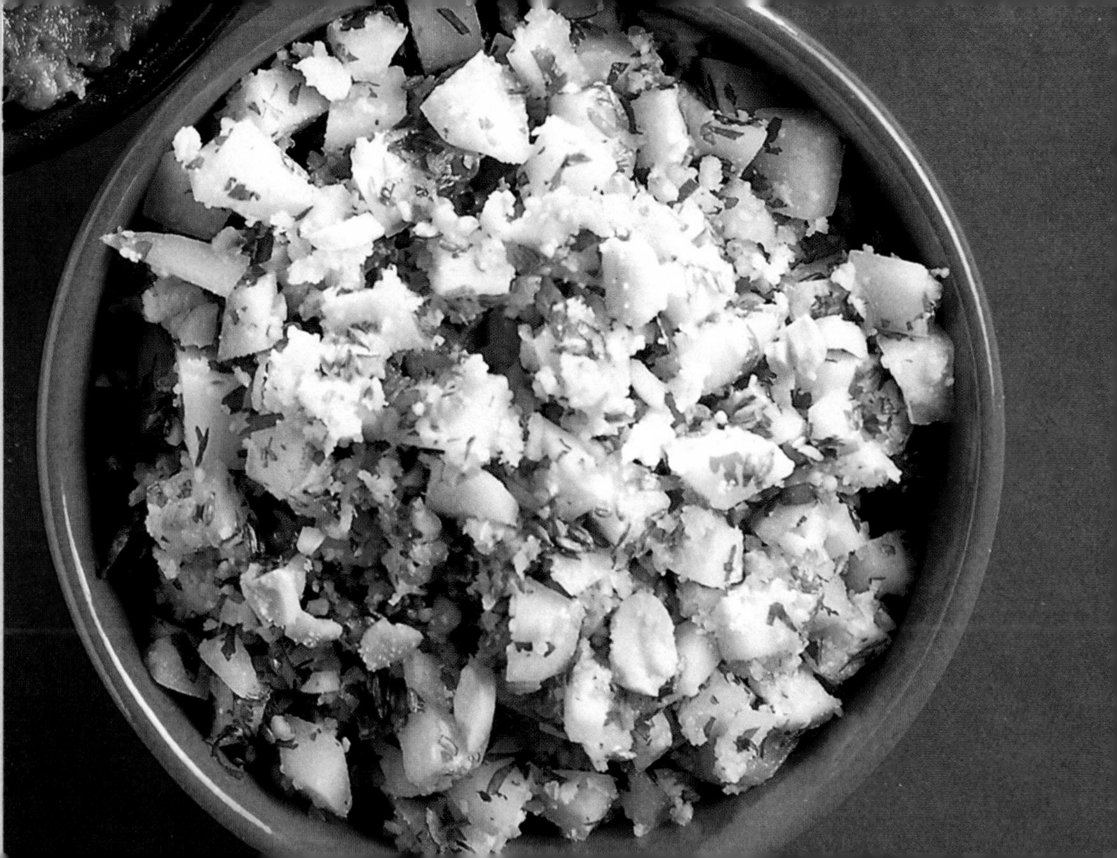

Khamang Kakdi

KHAMANG KAKDI

INGREDIENTS

Cucumbers .... 3 medium sized
Green chillies 2
Fresh coriander leaves ....
........................½ medium bunch
Peanuts (roasted and peeled) ... ½ cup
Coconut (scraped) .... 1/3 cup
Lemon juice .... 1 tbsp

Sugar .... 1 tsp
Salt .... to taste
For tempering
Pure *ghee* .... 1 tbsp
Mustard seeds .... ½ tsp
Cumin seeds .... ¼ tsp

METHOD OF PREPARATION

1   Peel, wash, halve, deseed and finely chop cucumbers.
2   Remove stems, wash and finely chop green chillies. Clean, wash and finely chop coriander leaves. Crush roasted peanuts to a coarse powder.
3   Mix cucumbers with green chillies, peanut powder, scraped coconut, lemon juice and sugar.
4   Heat *ghee* in a small pan, add mustard seeds and let them crackle. Add cumin seeds, stir-fry briefly and add this tempering to the cucumber mixture and mix well.
5   Mix salt and serve immediately, garnished with chopped coriander leaves.

GAJAR AUR KISHMISH KA SALAD

INGREDIENTS

Carrots .... 4-5 large sized
Raisins .... ½ cup
Green chilli 1
Fresh mint leaves .... 6 – 8
Lemon juice .... 2 tbsps
Peppercorns (crushed) .... ¼ tsp

Honey .... 1 tbsp
Salt .... to taste
Black salt .... ¼ tsp
Walnut kernels (crushed) 6
Oil .... 1 tsp

METHOD OF PREPARATION

1   Peel, wash and thickly grate carrots. Refrigerate till use.
2   Wash, remove stalks of raisins and pat them dry. Remove stem, wash and finely chop green chilli. Clean and wash mint leaves and keep aside for garnishing.
3   Combine lemon juice, crushed peppercorns, green chilli, honey, salt, black salt, walnuts, raisins and oil to make a dressing.
4   Just before serving add dressing to grated carrots and toss. Serve garnished with mint leaves.

MINTED MUSHROOMS

INGREDIENTS

Mushrooms..... 20-24 medium sized	Fresh mint leaves .... 1 medium bunch
Lemon juice .... 2 tbsps	Skimmed milk yogurt ..... 3 tbsps
Tomato .... 1 medium sized	Salt .... to taste
Cucumber .... 1 medium sized	Cabbage or lettuce leaves ..... 4 to 5

METHOD OF PREPARATION

1 Clean and wash mushrooms and cut into quarters.
2 Place mushrooms in a thick-bottomed vessel along with lemon juice and a little salt. Stew them over low heat for ten minutes. Keep aside.
3 Wash, halve, deseed tomato and cut into one centimeter sized pieces. Peel, wash cucumber and cut it into one centimeter sized pieces. Clean, wash mint leaves, reserve one or two sprigs for garnishing and chop the rest.
4 Combine mushrooms with tomato, cucumber and chopped mint. Mix in skimmed milk yogurt and salt and toss lightly.
5 Serve on a bed of cabbage leaves or lettuce leaves garnished with a sprig of mint leaves.

PENNE IN THOUSAND ISLAND

INGREDIENTS

Penne (tubular pasta)	1 cup	Broccoli	¼ small sized
Cherry tomatoes	10-12	French beans	3-4
Capsicum	½ medium sized	Stuffed olives	4-5
Onion	1 medium sized	Oil	1 tbsp
Carrot	1 medium sized	Thousand Island Dressing	½ cup

CHEF'S TIP

In case of non availability of cherry tomatoes, use normal tomatoes cut into half inch sized pieces.

METHOD OF PREPARATION

1 Take three cups of water in a pan, add a little salt and bring it to a boil. Add penne pasta and cook for six to eight minutes on high heat or until almost cooked. Drain, remove and refresh penne with cold water. Mix in one tablespoon of oil and spread on a plate.

2 Wash cherry tomatoes. Wash, deseed and cut capsicum into one inch sized triangular pieces. Peel, wash, cut onion into quarters and

separate the layers. Peel, wash and cut carrot into one inch sized pieces. Wash and break broccoli into small florets. String, wash and cut French beans diagonally into one inch sized pieces.

3   Heat two cups of water in a pan, add carrot, broccoli and French beans. Cook on medium heat for three to four minutes. Remove and refresh with cold water and drain off excess water.

4   In a large salad bowl toss all the prepared vegetables along with pasta, cherry tomatoes and stuffed olives.

5   Add Thousand Island Dressing, lightly toss and serve cold.

HEALTHY SALAD IN GARLIC DRESSING

INGREDIENTS

Spinach .... 16-20 leaves
Lettuce .... 16-20 leaves
Red capsicum .... 1 medium sized
Tomatoes .... 4 medium sized
Pineapple .... 4 slices
Baby corns 6-8
Garlic .... 8-10 cloves

Malt vinegar .... 2 tbsps
Virgin olive oil .... 1 tbsp
Mustard paste .... 1 tbsp
Salt .... to taste
Pepper powder .... ¼ tsp
Brown sugar .... 1 tsp

METHOD OF PREPARATION

1   Clean and wash spinach and lettuce leaves under running water thoroughly. Drain and tear them roughly.

2   Wash and wipe dry red capsicums. Apply very little oil on it and

roast in a very hot oven till blisters form on the surface. Alternatively you can roast red capsicum on an open flame also. Cool a little and peel off top skin. Halve capsicum, deseed and cut into one and a half inch long strips.

3   Wash and cut tomatoes into halves and deseed. Cut them into one and a half inch long strips. Cut pineapple slices into one and a half inch long strips.

4   If the baby corns are tender, cut them into two and cut them into strips and use raw. Otherwise, blanch them in salted water for five to seven minutes, cool and cut them into two and cut them into strips.

5   Peel, wash and chop garlic. Combine malt vinegar, virgin olive oil, garlic, mustard paste, salt, pepper powder and brown sugar.

6   Mix red capsicum, baby corn, tomatoes and pineapple. Gently mix it with lettuce and spinach leaves. Pour prepared dressing onto the salad and toss well. Serve cold.

PINEAPPLE WALDORF

INGREDIENTS

Pineapple slices 3
Walnut kernels .... ½ cup
Celery .... 1 stalk
Lettuce .... 1 bunch

Mayonnaise .... 3 tbsps
Fresh cream .... 2 tbsps
Salt .... to taste
Peppercorns (crushed) .... ½ tsp

METHOD OF PREPARATION

1 Cut pineapple slices into half inch sized pieces.
2 Toast walnut kernels in the oven or on the *tawa* till a little crisp. Roughly break them into small pieces. Using a rolling pin crush a few walnuts to a coarse powder.
3 Wash, trim and cut celery stalk into half-inch sized pieces. Trim and thoroughly wash lettuce leaves and tear them into bite sized pieces.
4 Place pineapple, lettuce and toasted walnuts in a deep mixing bowl. Add mayonnaise and fresh cream.
5 Add salt to taste and freshly crushed pepper. Lightly toss the salad so that the dressing evenly coats the pineapple, walnuts and lettuce leaves.
6 Garnish with coarse walnut powder and serve cold.

Pineapple Waldorf

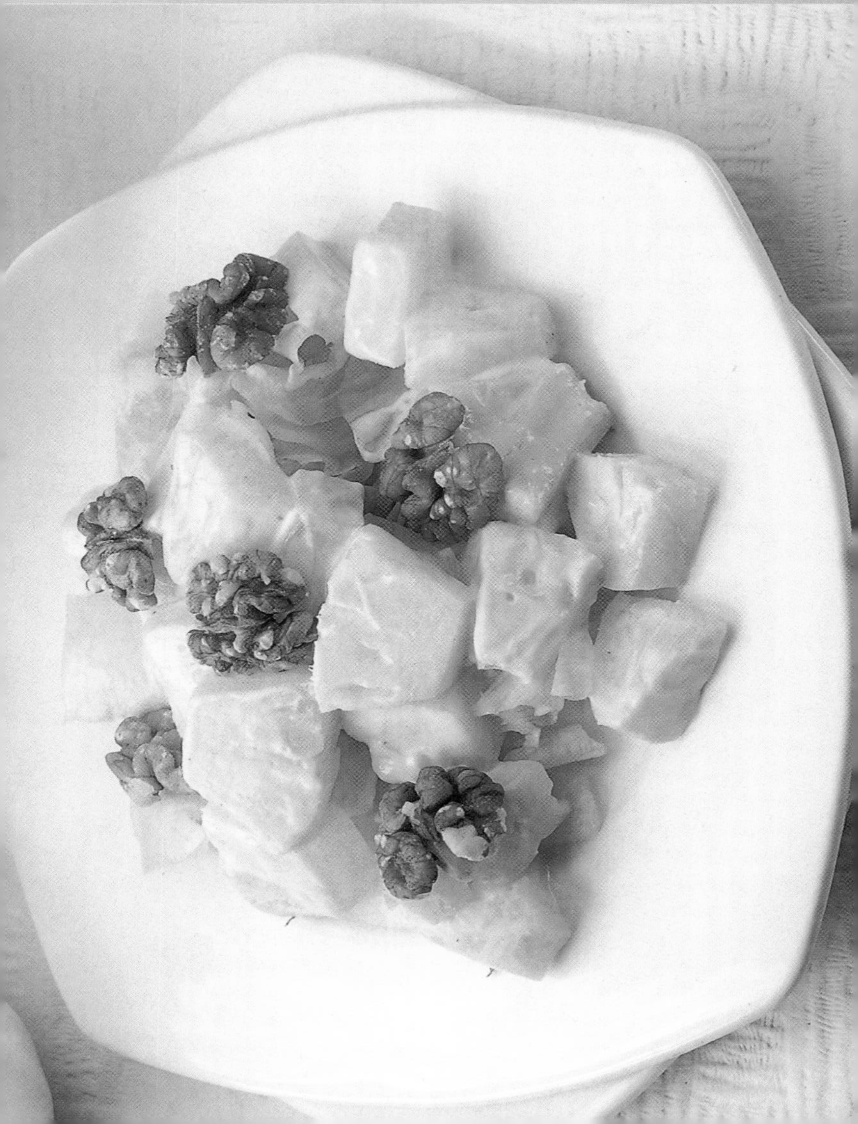

Three Chilli Potato Salad

THREE CHILLI POTATO SALAD

INGREDIENTS

Baby potatoes	16-18	Sugar	1 tsp
Oil	1 tbsp	Salt	to taste
Green chillies	2-3	Green peppercorns	10-12
Fresh coriander leaves	a few sprigs	Red chilli flakes	2 tsps
Lemon juice	2 tbsps	Tomato ketchup	1 tbsp

METHOD OF PREPARATION

1 Pre heat the oven to 180°C. Scrub and wash baby potatoes well, prick with a fork, apply oil. Roast potatoes in pre-heated oven at 180°C for thirty to forty minutes or till done.

2 Remove stems, wash, deseed and chop green chillies. Clean, wash and finely chop coriander leaves.

3 Cut potatoes in halves when done with skin still on.

4 In a bowl take lemon juice, sugar, salt, red chilli flakes, green chillies, green peppercorns and tomato ketchup. Mix well.

5 Add potatoes and toss. Serve salad garnished with chopped coriander leaves.

CHEF'S TIP

Use freshly crushed peppercorns as a substitute for green peppercorns.

MOONG MAUTH CHAAT

INGREDIENTS

Green gram (*moong*) (sprouted) .... 1 cup
Mauth (sprouted) .... 1 cup
Salt .... to taste
Turmeric powder ..... a generous pinch
Onion .... 1 small sized
Tomato .... 1 small sized
Capsicum .... 1 small sized

Green chillies 2
Raw mango .... 1 small sized
Roasted cumin seeds .... ¼ tsp
Red chilli powder .... ¼ tsp
Dried mango powder (*amchur*) .. 1 tsp
Oil .... 1 tbsp
Lemon juice .... 2 tsps
Chaat masala .... 2 tsps

METHOD OF PREPARATION

1   Boil *moong* and *mauth* sprouts separately in two cups of water each with a pinch of salt and a pinch of turmeric powder for about three to four minutes. Drain immediately and leave them in a colander

so that the water drains away completely.

2   Peel, wash and finely chop onion. Wash and chop tomato. Wash, halve, deseed and chop capsicum. Remove stems, wash and finely chop green chillies. Peel, wash and grate raw mango.

3   Mix sprouted *moong* and *mauth* with onion, capsicum, tomato, green chillies, roasted cumin seeds, red chilli powder, *amchur* powder, grated raw mango and oil.

4   Mix lemon juice, *chaat masala* and salt and pour over salad. Mix well and serve immediately.

Note: *Mauth* is brown coloured gram which is a little smaller in size to the green gram (*moong*). It is generally sprouted and used. It is known as *matki* in Maharashtra where *matki chi ussal* is a very popular dish.

FRUIT CHAAT

INGREDIENTS

Papaya .... 1 medium sized
Kiwi fruits .... 2 medium sized
Pomegranate ...... 1 medium sized
Orange .... 1 medium sized
Sweet lime .... 1 medium sized
Apples .... 2 medium sized

Pear .... 1 medium sized
Red chilli powder .... ½ tsp
Chaat masala .... 1 tbsp
Salt .... to taste
Lemon juice .... 1 tbsp

METHOD OF PREPARATION

1 Wash, peel and cut papaya and kiwi fruits into one inch sized cubes. Peel and separate pearls of pomegranate. Peel and cut orange and sweet lime into quarters. Wash and cut apples and pear into one inch sized cubes.

2 Put all the fruits into a large bowl. Add red chilli powder, *chaat masala*, salt and lemon juice. Mix well.

3 Serve cold.

GREENS AND CHEESE IN BALSAMIC DRESSING

INGREDIENTS

Red capsicums... 2 medium sized
Yellow capsicums .... 2 medium sized
Celery .... 2 stalks
Broccoli .... ½ medium sized
Fresh button mushrooms 6-7
Cucumber .... 1 medium sized
Iceberg/lolorosso lettuce .... 3–4 leaves
Walnut kernels .... ½ cup

Cheese .... 100 gms
Garlic .... 2-3 cloves
Salt .... to taste
Mustard seeds .... ½ tsp
Olive oil .... 4 tbsps
Balsamic vinegar .... 2 tbsps
Peppercorns (crushed) .... ¼ tsp
Honey .... 1 tbsp

METHOD OF PREPARATION

1 Wash and pat dry red and yellow capsicums. Roast them on open

fire till their skin gets charred. Immediately put them in cold water. Remove the charred skin, halve, deseed and cut into one inch sized cubes.

2 Trim, wash and slice celery. Wash broccoli, break into florets and blanch in two cups of boiling salted water for two to three minutes. Drain and refresh. Clean, wash and halve button mushrooms.

3 Wash, peel, halve, deseed cucumber. Cut into one inch sized cubes.

4 Wash and dry iceberg or lolorosso lettuce and tear roughly.

5 Toast walnut kernels. Cut cheese into one inch sized cubes.

6 Peel and wash garlic cloves. Pound them with salt, mustard seeds and olive oil and make a paste.

7 Mix the freshly ground paste with balsamic vinegar. Mix well and add freshly crushed peppercorns. Add honey and mix well.

8 Toss together the prepared vegetables and cheese cubes.

9 Just before serving add dressing and toss well.

TABBOULEH

INGREDIENTS

Cracked wheat *(burghul)* .... 4 tbsps
Fresh parsley ... 1 medium bunch
Spring onions 4
Fresh mint leaves 6-8
Tomato .... 1 medium sized

Lemon juice .... 1 tbsp
Salt .... to taste
Pepper .... to taste
Olive oil .... 2 tsps

METHOD OF PREPARATION

1   Soak the *burghul* for about fifteen minutes. Drain.
2   Clean, wash and roughly chop fresh parsley. Trim, wash and chop spring onions and greens separately. Clean, wash, dry and finely chop mint leaves.
3   Wash and wipe dry tomato. Quarter it, deseed and cut into half inch sized cubes.
4   Place *burghul* in a bowl. Add spring onions and mix, crushing onions slightly with your fingers.

5   Add parsley and mix well.
6   Add spring onion greens, mint leaves and tomato cubes.
7   To make the dressing, mix lemon juice, salt and pepper. Add it to the salad and mix.
8   Add olive oil, toss and chill salad before serving.

KACHUMBER SALAD

INGREDIENTS

Tomatoes .... 2 medium sized
Cucumbers .... 2 medium sized
Carrot .... 1 medium sized
Onion .... 1 large sized
White radish ...... 1 medium sized

Capsicum .... 1 medium sized
Green chillies 2
Fresh coriander leaves .... 2-3 sprigs
Lemon juice .... 1 tsp
Salt .... to taste

METHOD OF PREPARATION

1 Wash tomatoes and cut into half-inch sized pieces.
2 Wash, peel and cut cucumbers, carrot, onion and radish into half-inch sized pieces.
3 Wash, halve, deseed capsicum and cut into half-inch sized pieces.
4 Remove stems, wash green chillies and chop finely. Clean, wash and chop coriander leaves.
5 Mix all the vegetables. Add green chillies, coriander leaves, lemon juice and salt. Toss well.
6 Arrange in a salad bowl and serve cold.

INSALATA NUOVA CUCINA

INGREDIENTS

Iceberg lettuce .... 5-6 leaves
Fresh button mushrooms 6-7
Fresh yellow pimento .... 1 medium sized
Fresh red pimento ...... 1 medium sized
Tomatoes .... 2 medium sized
French beans 10-12
Asparagus (tinned) .... ¼ cup
Artichoke hearts (tinned) ..... ¼ cup

Stuffed green olives 8
For the dressing
Balsamic vinegar .... 2 tbsps
Olive oil .... 4 tbsps
Peppercorns (crushed) ... to taste
Salt .... to taste
Fresh basil sprigs .... to garnish

METHOD OF PREPARATION

1   Wash, drain and tear lettuce leaves roughly. Clean, wash mushrooms. Drain well and cut into quarters. Wash, pat dry yellow and red pimentos and dice them into half inch sized pieces. Wash and wipe dry tomatoes and chop into one-inch sized pieces. Wash and string French beans. Parboil in one cup of water until just tender. Drain and dice into half inch sized pieces. Cut asparagus and artichoke hearts into half inch sized pieces.

2   Mix all the vegetables together. Add stuffed olives. For dressing mix balsamic vinegar, olive oil, crushed peppercorns and salt.

3   Pour over the vegetables and toss thoroughly to mix. Garnish with fresh basil strips.

BEAN-SPROUTS AND FRUIT SALAD

INGREDIENTS

Bean sprouts .... 1 cup
Baby tomatoes 8
Oranges 2
Pineapple .... 2 slices
Mango (ripe) 1
Apple 1
Peach 1

Apricots 6
Lettuce leaves 6
Olive oil .... 4 tbsps
Balsamic vinegar .... 1 tbsp
Salt .... to taste
Peppercorns (freshly ground) ..... ½ tsp
Fresh orange juice .... 2 tbsps

METHOD OF PREPARATION

1   Wash and drain bean sprouts. Wash and cut baby tomatoes into two.
2   Peel oranges, separate segments, remove pips and slice them. Cut pineapple slices into cubes. Wash and peel mango. Cut into slices and then into cubes. Wash apple and peach and cut into cubes.

Soak apricots in warm water for a few hours, if dry or else wash and use as such. Wash lettuce leaves well under running water and shred.

3   Put all the above in a salad bowl. Add bean sprouts and toss.

4   Prepare dressing by mixing together olive oil, balsamic vinegar, salt, freshly ground peppercorns, fresh orange juice. Mix well and chill till use.

5   Just before serving add dressing to bean sprouts and fruit mixture and serve.

TOMATO MOZZARELLA AND OLIVE SALAD

INGREDIENTS

Tomatoes .... 2 medium sized
Mozzarella cheese .... 75 gms
Fresh basil .... a few leaves
Black olives 6
Green stuffed olives 6

Garlic .... 3 cloves
Peppercorns (crushed) .... 1 tsp
Salt .... to taste
Extra virgin olive oil .... 2 tsps
Lemon juice .... 1 tsp

METHOD OF PREPARATION

1 Wash and cut tomatoes into two centimeter thick slices. Slice mozzarella cheese into two centimeter thick slices.

2 Arrange alternate slices of tomatoes and mozzarella cheese in a platter.

3 Wash, wipe dry basil leaves. Arrange them between the tomato and cheese slices. Keep the rest in the centre. Wash and deseed black olives.

4 Add black and green olives to the platter.
5 Peel, wash and crush garlic. Add crushed peppercorns, salt, olive oil and lemon juice to it. Mix well.
6 Pour dressing over the salad and serve cold.

FOUR BEAN SALAD

INGREDIENTS

Green gram (*sabut moong*) .... ¼ cup
White cow beans (*chowli*) ..... ¼ cup
Red kidney beans (*rajma*) ..... ¼ cup
French beans 10-12
Onion .... 1 medium sized
Fresh coriander leaves ....
.... ½ medium bunch

Fresh mint leaves ....
.... ¼ medium bunch
Green chillies 2
Ginger .... 1 inch piece
Lemon juice .... 3 tbsps
Chaat Masala .... 1½ tsps

METHOD OF PREPARATION

1   Pick and wash white cow beans and kidney beans separately.
2   Soak them, separately, overnight in one cup of water each. Wash and soak green gram for about two hours.
3   Boil these soaked beans separately in salted water till soft. Drain and let cool.
4   String French beans, wash and cut into one-fourth inch sized pieces.

Boil in salted water till done. Drain immediately (you may reserve the cooking liquid for using as stock for some other recipe) and refresh with cold water. Drain and keep aside.

5 Peel, wash and cut onion into one-fourth inch sized pieces. Clean, wash, drain and chop coriander and mint leaves. Remove stems, wash and chop green chillies finely. Peel, wash and chop ginger.

6 Dilute lemon juice with equal amount of water. Stir in chopped coriander leaves, mint leaves, green chillies, ginger and *chaat masala*. Shake well and refrigerate the dressing for at least an hour.

7 Mix cooked beans with onion and add dressing. Toss salad to evenly mix the dressing.

Four Bean Salad

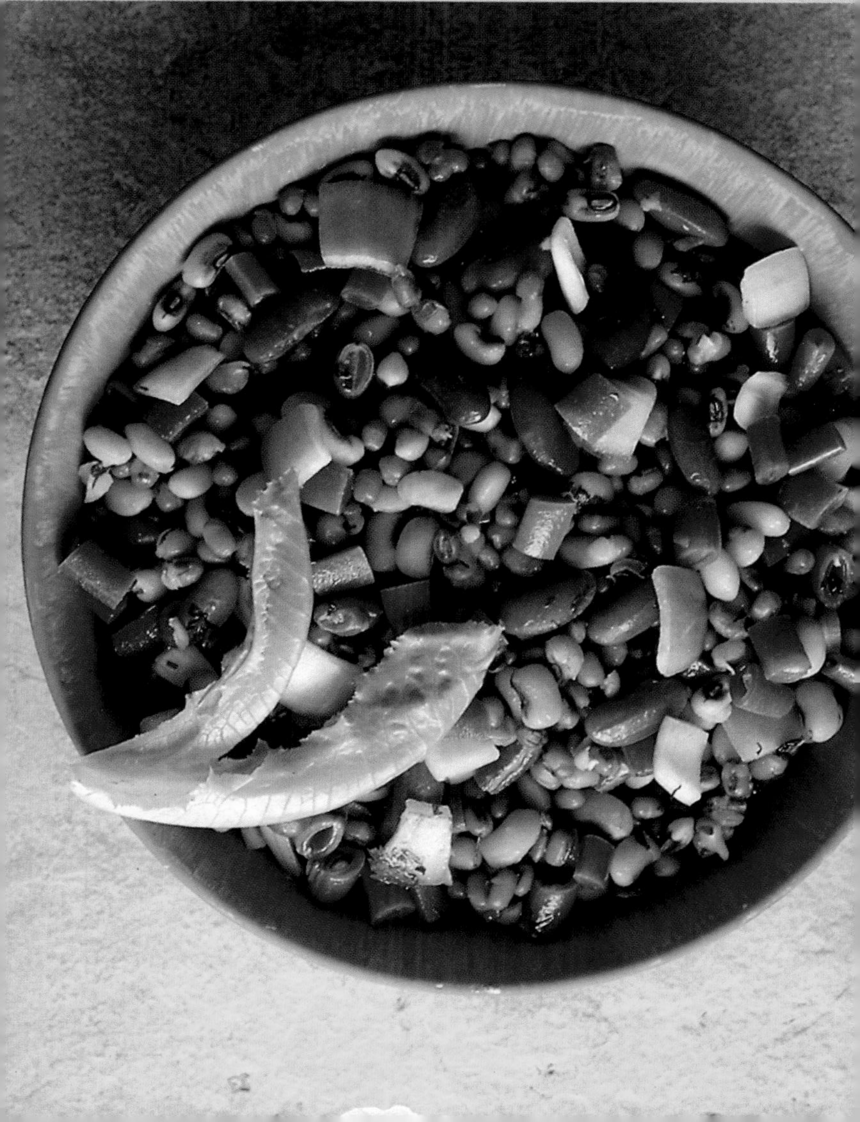

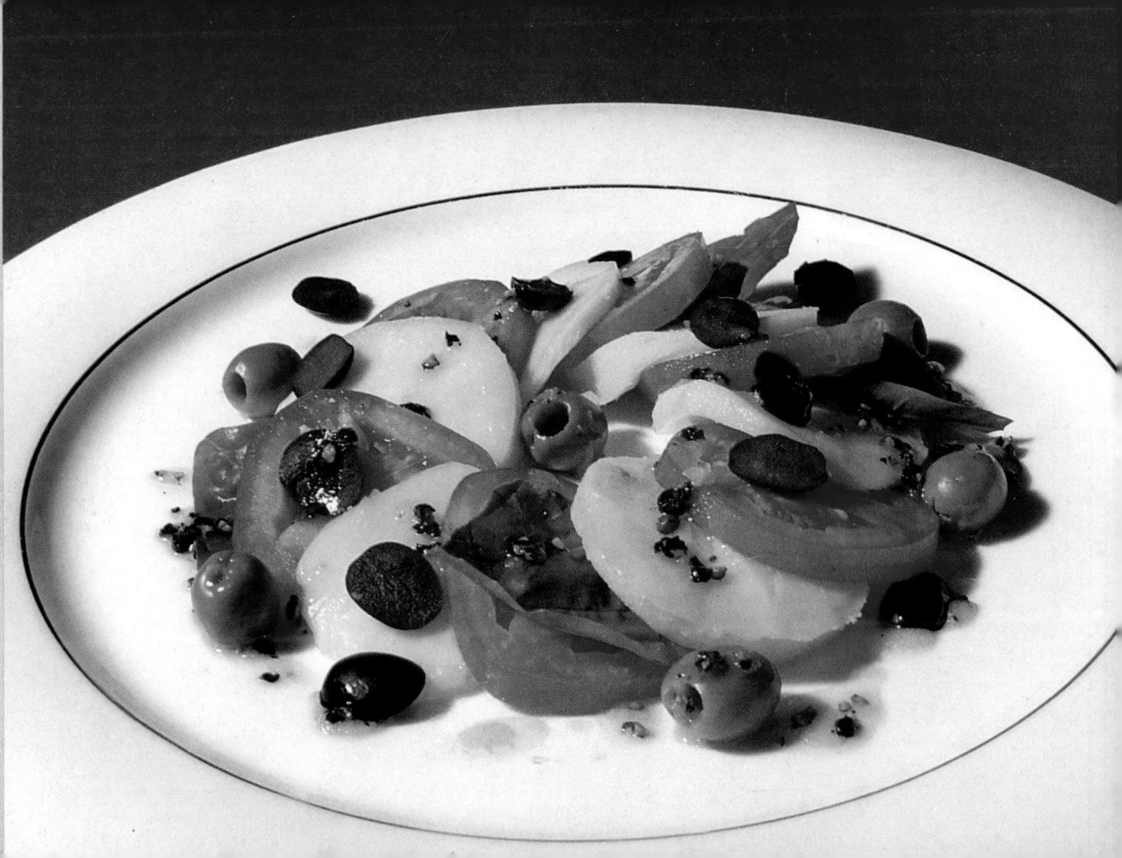

Tomato Mozarella and Olive Salad